ADVENTURES IN ANCIENT CHINA

Written by **Linda Bailey**
Illustrated by **Bill Slavin**

Kids Can Press

For my friend Barbara Knox, who had adventures of her own in China — L.B.

For Natalia, who loves to travel this big, beautiful world — B.S.

Acknowledgments
The author and illustrator are grateful to Dr. Chen Shen, Bishop White
Curator of Far Eastern Archaeology at the Royal Ontario Museum, who reviewed
the manuscript and art for accuracy and who was unfailingly helpful and
generous with his time. We would also like to thank Wang Qijun for sharing
his expertise on ancient Chinese architecture and furniture.

Thanks are due as always to the marvellous team at Kids Can Press, especially
Val Wyatt, editor, and Julia Naimska, designer.

Finally, thanks again to the book's first reader, Nico Lauck-Stephenson, for his help and suggestions.

Kids Can Press acknowledges the financial support of the Ontario Arts Council, the Canada Council for the Arts
and the Government of Canada, through the BPIDP, for our publishing activity.

Published in Canada by
Kids Can Press Ltd.
29 Birch Avenue
Toronto, ON M4V 1E2

Published in the U.S. by
Kids Can Press Ltd.
2250 Military Road
Tonawanda, NY 14150

www.kidscanpress.com

The artwork in this book was rendered in pen and ink and watercolor.
The text is set in Veljovic Book.

Edited by Valerie Wyatt
Designed by Julia Naimska
Printed and bound in Hong Kong, China, by Book Art Inc., Toronto

The hardcover edition of this book is smyth sewn casebound.
The paperback edition of this book is limp sewn with a drawn-on cover.

CM 03 0 9 8 7 6 5 4 3 2 1
CM PA 03 0 9 8 7 6 5 4 3 2 1

National Library of Canada Cataloguing in Publication Data

Bailey, Linda, 1948–
Adventures in ancient China / written by Linda Bailey ; illustrated by Bill Slavin.

(Good Times Travel Agency)
ISBN 1-55337-453-3 (bound).   ISBN 1-55337-454-1 (pbk.)

1. China — Civilization — 221 B.C.–960 A.D. — Juvenile literature. I. Slavin, Bill II. Title.
III. Series: Bailey, Linda, 1948– . Good Times Travel Agency.

DS747.42.B33 2003   j931   C2002-905546-6

Kids Can Press is a *corus*™ Entertainment company

The Binkerton kids would never have gone into the Good Times Travel Agency if it hadn't been for the noodles.

Well, who would? Good Times was an awful place — dark and dreary and deathly quiet. The windows were coated with thick gray grime. Cobwebs hung from the door. It made your skin prickle just to look.

Josh and Emma, the twins, did their best *not* to look. They'd been foolish enough to go through that door before. They *knew* what waited inside. But their sister Libby loved Chinese noodles more than anything. So when she smelled them from a block away, there was no stopping her!

LIBBY, WAIT!

Come back! We'll buy you a hot dog.

The twins followed Libby, and Libby followed her nose — right through the Good Times doorway!

Julian T. Pettigrew, the owner, was sitting in his usual place.

5

The smell of fried noodles was so heavenly that Josh and Emma forgot their caution. Surely it couldn't hurt to have one little taste.

Er … could I have a fork, please?

Mmmm … grblicious!

Take your time. Enjoy!

The moment they were finished, Josh and Emma thanked Mr. Pettigrew and headed for the door. Unfortunately, the old man was a little hard-of-hearing.

Yes, we love Chinese noodles.

Love Chinese travels?

Thanks, that was great!

Rummaging through his bookshelf, he pulled out a travel guidebook.

I'm getting a bad feeling.

Just ... don't ... open ... the book!

Julian T. Pettigrew's Personal Guide to ANCIENT CHINA

Open this book and your journey's begun. Read every word and your journey is done.

When Pettigrew offered the Guidebook to Libby, all three Binkertons grabbed for it — and all three missed! The book flew into the air. The pages fluttered open. There was a terrible, wonderful flash and ...

... the thing that they didn't want to happen, happened. The Binkertons were in a place — and a time — that was very, very, *very* far from home.

Barbarians?

JULIAN T. PETTIGREW'S PERSONAL GUIDE TO ANCIENT CHINA

WELCOME to ancient China! You have traveled back 2000 years and arrived during the Han dynasty (202 B.C. to A.D. 220). A dynasty is a ruling family. At the time of your visit, a Han emperor rules China.

Take a good look around. You're in the middle of a very old, very large empire. Did I say "middle"? The people here call their land "the Middle Kingdom." They believe it's the middle of the whole universe — and the center of all civilization, too.

China is definitely an *old* civilization. People have lived in its central river valleys for more than half a million years. They've been farming here for at least 9000 years. And while other civilizations come and go, China will remain unified under the rule of emperors for over 2000 years (221 B.C. to A.D. 1911), making it the longest continuous empire in world history.

It's also very big! Don't expect to see it all on your first visit. Ancient China is so big it has whole different climates in different regions. It's isolated, too — cut off from the rest of the world by deserts, mountains and the sea. Other civilizations are far away, and the ancient Chinese don't know (or care) much about them.

Maybe that's why the ancient Chinese see outsiders as not quite civilized. They think of people who live beyond their borders as "barbarians."

In case you haven't noticed ... that means YOU!

Josh had a soccer game and wanted to get home as quickly as possible. But Emma was beginning to feel curious.

We just race through the book, and we're out of here.

But now that we've come this far …

Barbarians?

Must be.

Even the closest of twins fight now and then. And that's exactly what this was — now *and* then!

I told you we shouldn't walk past the travel agency!

Well you were in such a big hurry to get home.

Definitely barbarians!

The argument went on so long that even the peasants got bored.

And on our fifth birthday, you got all the —

Libby? WHERE'S LIBBY?

In a WHAT? With a WHO? Going WHERE?

In a carriage. With an official. Going to the capital.

Libby had vanished. Not even a footprint left behind.

Josh and Emma raced around the rice paddies, trying to find someone — anyone! — who had seen her.

FARMING IN ANCIENT CHINA

Start your holiday by touring the countryside. Most of ancient China is countryside. Farming is an extremely important activity here.

Unfortunately, it's also a risky activity. In ancient China, you can never count on the rain. Often there's too much (flood) or too little (drought). Floods and droughts mean disasters for crops, and farmers sometimes have to borrow money they can't pay back. They may end up losing their land, their possessions and even their children. In a bad year, thousands of people may starve.

What do Chinese farmers grow? In the south, the main crop is rice, grown in watery fields called paddies. In the north, where it's colder, they grow wheat and a grain called millet. Farmers also grow vegetables and hemp (for cloth).

The Chinese don't raise pasture animals such as cows, so they don't have manure to fertilize crops. They use "night soil" (human waste) instead. Somebody has to empty the farm toilets into carts and take the night soil to spread on the fields. (Hint: If you're helping the farmer, try not to get this job.)

The capital, Chang'an, was days away to the north, and Libby had a huge head start. Josh and Emma set out after her, traveling as quickly as possible. In other words, not quickly at all.

When they were offered rides, they couldn't afford to be fussy. Even carts and wheelbarrows would do.

Traveling by water was faster ... but not much.

Dragons!

Dragons? Wait a minute, there's no such thing. Right, Emma?

Right ...

... I think.

TRAVEL IN ANCIENT CHINA

Traveling here can be tricky. Most roads are little more than cart tracks. When it rains, they turn into muddy bogs. Also, there's not much choice in vehicles. You might find a wooden cart and a donkey or ox. But horses are reserved for the wealthy, who ride in fancy carriages with canopies. The most luxurious carriages belong to the emperor. He rides on roads reserved for his own personal use.

If you get desperate, try a wheelbarrow. This ancient Chinese invention, sometimes called the "wooden ox," isn't exactly speedy, but it can carry passengers in a pinch.

Better still, travel by boat. It's faster, easier and cheaper than land travel. China has many rivers, and canals have been dug to connect them.

P.S. If you happen to hear the word "dragon" on your travels, don't be alarmed. Dragons are not scary here. The Chinese think of them as wise, good and strong. They believe that dragons are rain spirits who live in lakes, rivers and seas, as well as in rain clouds.

13

Josh and Emmma were desperate to find Libby. But it had been a long time since lunch. Stopping at the next farm, the twins offered to work in return for food.

I feel like a hamster.

I'm hungry enough to eat a hamster. Pedal!

CHINESE INVENTIONS

The ancient Chinese are great inventors. You've already discovered one of their inventions — the wheelbarrow. It may not look like much, but it makes moving loads a lot easier. And if you want to move *water*, why not try the "dragon's backbone"? You just "pedal" an endless chain of wooden planks to lift the water uphill. Excellent for watering the crops!

Not impressed yet? The Chinese also discovered that if you attach a lodestone (magnetic rock) to a wooden fish and float it in water, the fish will point north-south. Presto — the first compass!

Or how about a seismograph? China is a land of earthquakes, and a brilliant Han scientist (Zhang Heng) invented this device to record earthquake activity.

Still not impressed? Well, what are you holding in your hands? Paper! Chinese invention. Printing! Another Chinese invention. How about umbrellas, kites, fishing reels, mechanical clocks and waterwheels? All Chinese inventions! You may have to hang around a few years (say, 800) to see the Chinese invent gunpowder and fireworks ...

But hey! What's your hurry?

If the twins could have seen their little sister, they might not have felt so worried. Libby was traveling with a rich and kindly government official named Ban Tuo.

ANCIENT CHINESE SOCIETY

In ancient China, the emperor rules! But not alone. He has thousands of officials helping him run the country. Officials are very important people in China. They dress in silk robes and ride in carriages. They are more educated than anyone else. Young men from high-ranking families all over the country study hard, hoping to become officials.

Below the officials are the peasant-farmers. Peasants get a lot of respect in ancient China — even if they're very poor. They're considered important because they produce the country's food.

Below the peasants come the craftspeople who make jewelry and weapons and so on. And below them are the merchants, who sell things. In ancient China, it's considered shameful to make money from other people, so merchants get very little respect. They aren't allowed to wear silk clothing or ride horses or carry weapons. On the bright side, they can get very, very rich!

At the bottom of society are the soldiers. They don't get much respect *or* much money.

15

While Josh and Emma slept out in the open ...

Poor Libby.

This is the last time I go anywhere without my sleeping bag.

ANCIENT CHINESE HOMES

Having trouble finding a place to sleep? Don't worry. You can always find a nice wall to huddle beside. The ancient Chinese love walls! They build them everywhere — around their fields, their houses, their cities and even around parts of their country.

But maybe you'll be lucky and get invited to stay in a wealthy home. There'll be a wall around it, of course. Enter through the gate. Inside, you'll find a courtyard — or maybe two, with the inner one reserved for family and close friends. The buildings are framed with wood. (Good thinking in this land of earthquakes! Wood is

... Libby slept in comfort in the homes of the rich.

You are most welcome to my humble home.

You must meet our charming little barbarian.

I'm a charmy barby. Tra la la!

Hee, hee, hee!

flexible and doesn't hurt as much as stone if it falls on you.)

The main building may be several stories high. Take a look inside. Notice how spacious and richly decorated the rooms are with silk hangings and painted screens. Settle down on the rug-covered floor. Lounge on one of the large embroidered cushions. Comfy? Enjoying yourself?

You'd feel very different in a poor person's house. Imagine being crammed in with your relatives day after day in a mud-plastered hut with a thatched roof. Think of how stuffy it would get in the winter as you put cloth over the windows and wrapped yourself in quilts to stay warm. As for the summer ... well, if you have any brains at all, you'll head outdoors, where there's room to breathe!

While Josh and Emma scrambled to feed themselves ...

Emma, look! I found an onion!

Is it big enough for two?

FOOD IN ANCIENT CHINA

Hungry? Find a place on the floor! The ancient Chinese eat at small low tables. All you need is a bowl and chopsticks. Food here is cut up into small bite-sized pieces so that you can pick it up easily. (Well, you *could* if you practiced.)

Grain is the main food — wheat, millet or rice. If you're rich, you'll eat plenty of other foods, as well. Try some geng (stew) made of meat and vegetables. The meat might be pig, deer, ox, sheep or even dog. The vegetables could be cabbage, garlic, leeks, yams or celery. There may also be some delicacies you're not used to, such as snake, turtle, baked owl or bear's paw. Yum!

... Libby dined in splendor among noble company.

Slurpy, burpy, yummy, tummy!

What is she saying? Hee, hee, hee.

I don't know, but she is very funny! Ha, ha, ha.

In case you're still hungry after all those dishes, the meal will end with fruit.

If you're poor, your meals will be simple. You'll get a bowl of grain and vegetable geng and ... that's it. Well, okay, you might get some beans, too — and an occasional bit of meat, if you raise chickens or pigs.

But here's the good news. You're here during the Han dynasty, and that's when the Chinese people invented — NOODLES! The cooks here make noodles by blending flour with water. They have no idea what they're starting. Spaghetti! Lasagna! Macaroni and cheese! If it weren't for the ancient Chinese, you might never have tasted any of these.

Day after day, Josh and Emma trudged north in their sister's tracks. One day, they stumbled across some people making paper ...

What's the big deal? We made paper at school.

Do you think grass would work?

How about hair?

Yeah, but here they're doing it for the first time — ever!

WRITING AND PAPER

The Chinese began writing a very long time ago (around 1300 B.C.). They began by drawing pictograms (small pictures) of what they wanted to say. As time went by, there were more and more pictograms, which got more and more complicated. Finally, there were thousands of different "characters" in the Chinese written language.

At first, the Chinese wrote on turtle shells, bones and bronze vessels. Later they wrote on strips of bamboo. These strips were read up and down and tied together with string to make a "book." Important messages would be written on silk instead. (Very expensive! Not for first drafts.)

It wasn't until the Han dynasty — hey, that's now! — that paper was invented. Credit is given to an official named Cai Lun in A.D. 105, but he probably just improved the process. The first papermakers used old rags to make their paper. Later they experimented with mulberry bark, rattan, bamboo and even fishnets.

Take a good look at the paper made here. It's one of the most important inventions ever. It will be hundreds of years before the rest of the world catches on!

... and the next day, they spotted some women making silk.

Are they making soup?

No. Silk!

EEK! BARBARIANS!

They must not find out the secret!

THE SECRET OF SILK

STOP! Don't read this. It's top secret! You could be tortured to death just for knowing.

What? Still reading? Well, don't say I didn't warn you.

The ancient Chinese have been making silk cloth for thousands of years. In all that time, they have been careful never to let the secret of how to make silk leave the country. But if you *must* know ...

Get yourself a whole lot of silkworms (caterpillars of silk moths). For a month or so, feed them mulberry leaves several times a day to make them grow.

Eventually, they will be ready to spin cocoons. Each cocoon is made up of a very long single strand of silk (up to 900 m or 3000 ft. long). When the cocoon is finished, drop it into boiling water (bad luck for the worm). The boiling water will make the silk strand unwind. Reel it in and twist it with other strands to make thread. Weave the thread into beautiful, strong, valuable silk cloth.

There! Now you know the secret of silk. ARE YOU OUT OF YOUR MIND? (P.S. Papermaking is a secret, too. You must like to live dangerously.)

21

Josh and Emma had no idea what the problem was ...

No, wait! We're not barbarians! We're really quite civilized.

Aiiee!

Eeeeeee!

Help!

... until Emma checked the Guidebook.

Help!

Aiiee!

Eeek!

Uh-oh. Silk's a big secret. And we're in really big trouble.

It had been a rough journey for the twins ... and now it got rougher.

Find the barbarians!

They must not leave China with the secret.

We're not barbarians!

I can't believe they're making such a fuss about worms!

Hours later, cold and miserable, the twins finally snuck away. Down the road, a kind woman took pity on them and invited them to spend the night with her family.

No noodles, thanks. They bring back ... er ... bad memories.

I don't suppose you have a fork?

FAMILIES IN ANCIENT CHINA

Families are extremely important in China, but they're probably different from *your* idea of a family. An ancient Chinese family includes not only relatives who are alive now, but also those who have died and those who are not yet born. Families worship their dead ancestors with prayers and offerings of food and drink. They believe that they must have sons to continue the family into the future. (Daughters don't count because they join their husbands' families.)

If you're a girl in ancient China, you'd better be the obedient type. When you're young, you'll have to obey your parents. When you get married, you'll have to obey your husband and *his* parents. You won't get to do much thinking and choosing for yourself.

But cheer up! Things will improve when you get old. Children in China are brought up to respect their parents and take care of them in old age. This is called filial piety. A famous example is a man named Laizi. He was so devoted to his old parents that even when he was seventy himself, he played with toys like a little boy, just to make his mother and father happy. Now *that's* filial piety!

23

Eventually, they reached the capital city, Chang'an. Taking a chance, they asked about their little sister.

Have you seen a small ... uh ...

... barbarian?

There! In the city. She went into the emperor's palace.

CITIES IN ANCIENT CHINA

What did I tell you? The ancient Chinese love walls! Whenever they build a city, they build a wall around it for defense. Notice the watchtowers where soldiers stand guard. There is also a moat for extra defense. At the first sign of danger, the bridge is removed and the huge gates are closed.

Inside the capital lives the emperor. His home is a magnificent palace with — guess what? — more walls around it. Actually, the palace is more like a "palace city" with many splendid buildings.

Surrounding the palace are government buildings and the homes of wealthy people. Ordinary people live jammed together in crowded streets near the market and main gates.

Warning: Ordinary people are not allowed inside the palace. This means you! The Chinese emperor lives a secluded life with his family, servants and courtiers. He's hardly even seen by ordinary people.

Stay away! Back off! KEEP OUT!

The next step was clear.

We can do it!

Yeah, sure. All we have to do is ... BREAK INTO THE EMPEROR'S PALACE?

Josh and Emma waited till night fell. Then, mustering their courage and using their best sneaking skills, they snuck into the city.

They snuck up to the palace.

They snuck *inside* the palace.

They snuck all over the palace and peeked into a hundred rooms.

Where the heck was Libby?

Youch! Are they torturing him?

No. Curing him.

Tsk, tsk, tsk ... too much yin ... not enough yang.

ANCIENT CHINESE MEDICINE

The ancient Chinese believe that there are two great forces in nature and in every human being — yin and yang. Yin is cold, dark, negative and female. Yang is warm, bright, positive and male. Yin and yang are opposites, but both are necessary.

Yin and yang are supposed to be in balance. If they're not, watch out! In nature, an imbalance can mean earthquakes, droughts, floods or other nasty happenings. In your body, an imbalance can make you ill.

If you get sick in ancient China, doctors will treat you by trying to balance your yin and yang. They might give you herbs or suggest changes in your diet. Or they might use acupuncture. This means they will insert thin needles into your body along lines called meridians to release the forces of yin and yang. Acupuncture is a very old treatment that continues to be used in modern times.

Go ahead. Lie down. Try it! It won't hurt.

(Much.)

27

All through the night, the twins continued their search, getting more nervous by the minute. The palace was huge! And not everyone was sleeping.

Where the heck was Libby?

Look! A disaster is coming.

Just one disaster? He ought to try *my* life!

ANCIENT CHINESE BELIEFS

If you happen to be out on a palace wall late at night, you might come across some ancient Chinese scholars studying the night sky. They watch it closely, looking for unusual events (such as comets), which they believe may be signs of coming disasters on Earth. The ancient Chinese believe that the universe, Earth and people are all closely connected and can affect one another. They also believe that everything in nature (winds, rivers, mountains) has a spirit, and they try to stay friendly with these spirits.

Unlike many civilizations, the ancient Chinese don't have a single religion. Instead, they follow the teachings of three great religious teachers of the 6th century B.C.:

Finally, in the wee hours of the night, Josh and Emma dropped off to sleep ... but not for long.

It's them!

The barbarians! The ones who know too much!

For the last time — we are *not* barbarians!

• Kong Zi, also known as Confucius, taught respect for other human beings, especially the "golden rule" — do to others what you would like them to do to you.
• Lao Zi taught that everyone should live by "the way" — surrender to nature instead of having rules and goals.
• The Buddha (born in northern India) taught that if you meditated and gave up worldly desires, you could get to a wonderful state called nirvana.

Together, the teachings of these three leaders are called "the three ways." The ancient Chinese believe that all these teachings are helpful in life. Most important is to keep things in balance. Just like yin and yang.

(You don't remember yin and yang? Turn back to page 27.)

Seconds later, the guards appeared. The twins were on the run again — straight into the emperor's throne room!

The good news was — they found Libby.

THE EMPEROR

Hoping to meet the emperor? Forget it! He's far too important for the likes of you. The ancient Chinese think of their emperor as the Son of Heaven. They believe he gets his right to rule from heaven itself. This right is called the Mandate of Heaven, and it gives the emperor a lot of power. His word is law. He has the power of life and death over his people.

But here's the catch. The emperor has the Mandate of Heaven only as long as he's a good ruler. If he's a

Scooping up their sister, the twins kept running. Behind them came … the whole imperial court!

weak or bad ruler, the heavens will show their displeasure through signs and disasters, and his reign (and that of his family) will end. A new Son of Heaven will take over. Through China's long history, ruling families come and go — the Shang, Zhou, Qin, Han, Sui and Tang dynasties, just to name a few.

A final word of advice: if you *insist* on meeting the emperor, make sure you get a personal invitation. This is not just good manners. Uninvited visitors are executed!

The Binkertons needed a safe place to hide — a place where no one would look.

The camel!

Tell me you're kidding.

Any more great ideas?

Shhh! I'm thinking.

The next thing the Binkertons knew, they were leaving the city. This was an excellent idea ... except where were they going?

THE SILK ROAD

Want the ride of a lifetime? Take a camel ride along the Silk Road. But do it at your own risk.

The Silk Road is a famous overland trade route from ancient China to the West. Traders carry valuable silk cloth (and other Chinese goods such as jade and spices) thousands of miles to Persia. It's a terrible trip! The route crosses high mountains, windswept plains and sun-baked deserts. In the daytime, travelers sweat and swelter. At night, they freeze. To make things worse, there are bandits along the way, waiting to attack.

It's so dangerous, traders travel in groups (caravans) for protection. Most traders don't travel the whole way. Instead, they do stretches, like a relay race.

Carrying the goods are the only animals tough enough to tolerate these conditions — camels. Camels can go long distances without food or water. They can smell water a long way off in the desert. They can survive sandstorms.

Important reminder: *you* are not a camel. So here's one last piece of advice. DON'T GO!

The camel wasn't exactly comfortable. But it carried them to a sight so amazing, Josh was finally glad they had come.

Wow! That's a great wall!

Exactly!

THE GREAT WALL

The Great Wall began as a number of smaller walls built over the centuries. These walls were joined together, and added to, by the first emperor of China (Qin dynasty, 221 to 207 B.C.), creating a Great Wall almost 6400 km (4000 mi.) long. The Han emperors who followed repaired the wall and made it even longer. In fact, the ancient Chinese often call it the Long Wall.

Great Wall

Silk Road

Chang'an

The purpose of this wall, located along the border, is to keep out the "barbarians" who live on the grassy plains north of China. All along the wall, Chinese soldiers stand guard in forts and watchtowers. When an attack comes, the soldiers signal the next tower with flags or torches. Soldiers also act as border guards, preventing criminals from leaving the country.

Most of the Great Wall is made of layers of earth, pounded to make it hard. Layers of reed or rubble make it stronger, and sometimes mud bricks are added on the outside. Centuries later, during the Ming dynasty, a much grander, fancier wall will be built of bricks. For now, dirt will have to do.

Even so, isn't it Great?

Emma read in the Guidebook that the Great Wall was at China's border. This was wonderful. Their troubles were nearly over.

We just have to cross the wall, and we're out of China!

I wonder if I can still make that soccer game.

But how to get across? The Binkertons waited for their chance. The first stairs they saw, they slipped down from their camel ... and ran!

GO! NOW!

Stay low!

Once again, the Binkertons were on the run!

I am getting *so* tired of this.

KITES

Tired of traveling? Need a break? Take some time off and go fly a kite!

Kites were invented in ancient China before the time of the Han dynasty. No one knows exactly where the idea came from. Some people say that a farmer's hat, held by a string, got caught in a gust of wind — and that was the first kite! Another suggestion is that a sail got away from a boat.

Early Chinese kites were used in warfare. One legend tells of a Chinese general who flew a kite over an enemy's palace and then

Once again, Libby surprised everyone.

Joshy, Emma! Look at me!

LIBBY!

NO!

measured the string to see how long a tunnel he would need to burrow under the walls. Another general flew kites above his enemies at night. The kites were built to make mysterious wailing sounds, which frightened the enemy soldiers so badly that they ran away. Kites were also used for signaling and spying.

Some ancient Chinese kites are large enough to carry a human into the air. This may sound like fun, but it's actually very dangerous and has even been used as a punishment for prisoners. Most of them crashed and died. (Not fun!)

The twins leaped after Libby, and ... all ... three ... slowly ... floated ... down.

The Binkertons were safe ...

Whew! I thought we were goners.

... except for the barbarians!

NOMADS OF THE NORTH

Who are these so-called "barbarians" anyway? Well, of course, to the ancient Chinese, all foreigners are barbarians. But the most troublesome barbarians of all are the nomadic (wandering) tribes who live to the north.

These nomads are very different from the ancient Chinese. Instead of living a settled farming life, they hunt and herd, roaming the northern steppes (grassy plains) in search of fresh grazing lands for their sheep and horses. And speaking of horses, these nomads are practically born on a horse. They ride like the wind! At night, they sleep in tents instead of houses.

They also have a bad habit of raiding and robbing Chinese settlements. This is a major problem for the ancient Chinese, who try everything to stop the nomads — trading with them, bribing them with silk, even offering them beautiful princesses as wives. And of course there's that Great big Wall.

In Han times, the horse-riding nomads are the Xiong-nu. Later in history, the Mongols will invade from the north — and even later, the Manchu. They are all quite scary, so for goodness' sake, stay out of their way. This is your very last warning!

The Binkertons tried to reason with them.

Stop! Wait! We're barbarians, too!

Yeah! We're on your side!

But the barbarians weren't very good listeners. Thundering full speed toward the Binkertons, they drove them right up the wall!

The kids got halfway up the kite rope and stopped.

Barbarians below! Chinese soldiers above! And in between ... a Binkerton wall hanging!

What a way to go.

At least we're together.

There was only one thing to do.

READ!

Would it work? Could they do it?

The situation was desperate! The Binkertons —

READ! READ! READ!

Ignoring Mr. Pettigrew's invitations, the Binkertons headed straight for the door.

Are you sure you won't hang around for a while?

They vowed they would never come near the Good Times Travel Agency again for the rest of their lives.

And if you see me eating a noodle, kick me!

But never? Well, that's a very long time.

Even for time travelers.

Julian T. P
Personal
to

ANCIENT CHINA

Fact or fantasy?

How much can you believe of *Adventures in Ancient China*? The story of the Binkertons and their adventures is just that — a story.

But there really was a time in ancient China when emperors ruled and silk was a secret and ... well, if you really want to know, read the Guidebook! That's where you'll find the facts. All the information in Julian T. Pettigrew's Personal Guide to Ancient China is based on historical fact.

More about ancient China

China has a long and fascinating history. Prehistoric people lived in caves in China more than half a million years ago, and by 9000 years ago, there were farming settlements. Later, during China's Bronze Age, the first of its great ruling families, the Shang dynasty (about 1600–1050 B.C.), built fortified cities in northern China.

But it wasn't until 221 B.C. that China was unified into an empire. That was when the leader of the Qin kingdom defeated other warring rulers and declared himself First Emperor of China. (Qin is pronounced "chin" in Chinese, and this is how China got its name.) The First Emperor was a harsh man, and his dynasty lasted less than fifteen years. Even so, he accomplished a great deal, including the linking and extension of many walls to create the Great Wall.

It was during the next dynasty (the Han dynasty) that the Binkertons visited China. This famous dynasty lasted more than 400 years (202 B.C. to A.D. 220), except for a short interruption when another leader held power. The Han dynasty was a time of progress, creativity and expansion. Literature flourished, and great works of history were written. The Silk Road was developed, and the civil service (a network of government officials) was firmly established. It was a period of great accomplishment and invention and is considered a high point of ancient Chinese civilization.

The Han dynasty was followed by 300 years of division and unrest before another dynasty (Sui) took control. Altogether the Chinese imperial system (rule by emperors) lasted for more than 2000 years, ending finally in 1911. During that time there were many dynasties. Some ruled for only a few decades, while others lasted for centuries, but through it all, China's central government and strong civil service endured.

If you're not sure where China is, take a look at the world map on this page. China is an enormous country — then and now. At the time that the Binkertons visited, it would have taken a very long time to trek across it — and an even longer time to travel the ancient Silk Road leading to the Western world.

Even so, there are plenty of historians who would love to make the trip! If only they could find the right travel agency ...

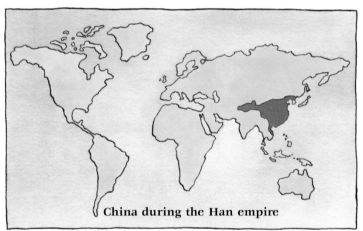

China during the Han empire

In this book